Spells & Rituals

USING CANDLE MAGICK

Sally Love

WARNING: READ THIS INFORMATION
Never place a candle on any unprotected surface that may be damaged by heat or dripping wax. Stand candles in containers capable of containing spillages of molten wax. Never touch or mover the candle when lit as it may become hot during use. Never leave a burning candle unattended. Never leave fragments of matches or wick in the candle after lighting as these may become a dangerous second source of flame. Burn candles away from walls and overhanging surfaces and away from draughts. Always keep burning candles away from flammable materials and never allow the candles flame to become enlarged, to avoid this trim the wick to a safe length between uses.

Published in 2001 by Caxton Editions
20 Bloomsbury Street
London WC1B 3JH
a member of the Caxton Publishing Group

© 2001 Caxton Publishing Group

Designed and produced for Caxton Editions
by Open Door Limited
Rutland, United Kingdom

Editing: Mary Morton
Coordination and Typesetting: Jane Booth
Digital Imagery © PhotoDisc Inc.

Title: Spells & Rituals Using Candle Magick
ISBN: 1 84067 343 5

Spells&Rituals

USING CANDLE MAGICK

Sally Love

CAXTON EDITIONS

4

CONTENTS

CONTENTS

INTRODUCTION TO A WITCH'S CANDLE MAGICK

HOW TO CREATE A MAGICKAL ENVIRONMENT IN YOUR HOME

Candle magick can be one of the simplest yet most effective forms of magick. You can simply light a white candle whilst making a wish or you could perform your own rituals, employing the magickal meanings of herbs and colours, or carving your own inscriptions into the side of the candle – there are many exciting methods to explore. Candle magick is both fun and powerful. You can see your spell working as the candle burns down over your inscriptions, or as the magickal herbs you have chosen crackle in the glowing flame.

This book will guide you through the various different methods you will need to know in order to create your own candle magick that is fun, safe and works! You will learn about the magick of herbs, oils, colours, how to employ the help of the elements and deities and how to create sacred space. I have also put together a few candle magick spells to get you started, and which will hopefully inspire you to begin creating your own magick. ENJOY!

Below: candle magick can be one of the simplest yet most effective forms of magick. You can simply light a white candle whilst making a wish.

CHECKLIST ON HOW TO BEGIN YOUR CANDLE MAGICK

Decide upon magick – ethics, ensure you are clear about intent

Choose your methods, i.e. herbs, oils, engraving, photos, colour candle

Prepare your working space (altar etc. with white candle)

Grounding

Cleanse your candle

Begin your ritual

WHAT IS MAGICK?

Magic is described in the Oxford English Dictionary as "1 supposed art of controlling things by supernatural power. 2 conjuring tricks."

You have probably noticed by now that I spell the word with a "k" on the end. I feel that "magic" refers to card tricks and conjuring rabbits out of hats (which I unfortunately can't do!) and "magick" refers to a far more powerful art, which you will begin learning to do here. To me, spelling the word differently ensures we know what kind of magic/magick we are talking about.

Below: simply put, magick, when used wisely, is the ability of the person performing it to use the power of their mind to help bring about a desired change.

Simply put, magick, when used wisely, is the ability of the person performing it to use the power of their mind to help bring about a desired change, alter a situation or to give a helping hand to someone in need.

*Left: an alter set out with all
the elements in place ready for
candle magick.*

All magick works but it may not always work how you want it to! For example, you should only do a spell for someone if they ask you to. Let's say you did a spell for a friend to recover from a bad cold quickly, without their knowledge. They were better the following day, so you triumphantly said it was your spell that worked the magick. To your surprise, they then blamed you for meddling. Had you thought that they may have needed the break? They could have been working day and night over the last year and it was nature's way of giving them some time to rest at home. Or they may have needed the time to think about where they are going in life, and so you prevented them from making the necessary changes that would have brought them more happiness.

Another example: you may do a spell simply saying "I need to move house" and find a few days later that the place you are living in is flooded and so you are forced to move. Or on a much more serious note, you do a spell asking for money and your favourite great aunt dies and leaves you an inheritance.

The moral of these stories is – be careful of what you ask for, as it may just come true!

As you can see from the above examples, you need to state very clearly what you want, making sure there is no room for misinterpretation.

So remember, only perform magick for someone else if they ask you to, or they give you their permission. If, after saying this, you still feel that you have to perform a spell for someone without them knowing, make sure that to the best of your knowledge it will benefit them, and ensure you say that if the spell is not meant to be and if it doesn't help them, it will not work.

There is a saying which needs to be employed every time you perform magick: "Do what thou wilt an it harm none". This means be ethical in what you are doing, have your desired outcome defined clearly and do not do any magick that will harm anyone else by altering their mind, body or spirit against their will.

As you saw from the first example, don't assume you know what a person wants or needs. Never perform magick that will harm someone else to bring you what you need or want in your life. So, if you have ever wondered what the difference between white magick and black magick is: black magick is going against the ethic "Do what thou wilt an it harm none"; "white magick" is working with this in mind.

This brings me neatly to some words of caution. Most magick you practise will come back on you in some way. So, if you practise "black magick", beware of the boomerang effect! What's the boomerang effect? Well, whatever magick you send out to someone carries a great possibility that it will come back on you threefold. If you perform magick with good intentions, great. But watch out if your intentions are not ethical! Some people are consciously or sub-consciously psychically protected. Therefore, if you perform any kind of magick towards someone with this protection around them, it will simply bounce off and come straight back to you - three times as powerful as you sent it out! My personal view is that, even if you psychically protect yourself and perform "black magick", the rules of Karma come into play – you lose your right to protection and you will eventually be caught out by your own actions. What goes around comes around!

Far left: "do what thou wilt an it harm none". This means be ethical in what you are doing, have your desired outcome defined clearly and do not do any magick that will harm anyone else by altering their mind, body or spirit against their will.

Below: there are differing opinions about whether to light your candle with a lighter or with matches — use whichever you feel drawn towards

Above: when you are working with magick you are tapping into the energy waves that are all around us and harnessing them, building the energy all around you and then releasing it into the atmosphere to bring forth your desire.

So, do what you want – we all have free will – but be prepared to either suffer or enjoy the consequences accordingly. Remember, what you to do others, the earth and the environment you do to yourself.

When you are working with magick you are tapping into the energy waves that are all around us and harnessing them, building the energy all around you and then releasing it into the atmosphere to bring forth your desire. The power of the mind is very strong and you will learn in this book ways in which you can "will" things to happen. Imagination and "will" feeds on our

inner child, and so carving symbols into a candle and singing or chanting, whilst performing magick, activates this inner child and enables us to focus solely upon what we are doing. No outside thoughts must enter your head when you are doing candle magick – remain entirely focused throughout. Think, feel and express yourself fully with good intent and you can't go wrong! There is a vast amount of information on magick for you to find out if you wish. I have kept it as simple as possible, highlighting all I feel you need to know at this point.

Most magickal practices incorporate the four elements of Earth, Air, Fire and Water within their rituals. These elements correspond with the astrological signs:

Earth signs: Taurus, Virgo, Capricorn
Air signs: Gemini, Libra, Aquarius
Fire signs: Aries, Leo, Sagittarius
Water signs: Cancer, Scorpio, Pisces.

Each of the elements is assigned to a particular compass direction, too. These directions do vary amongst various practices, but I use the following:

North = Earth
South = Fire
West = Water
East = Air.

Also, think about what each of the elements means to you. Some popular correspondences are: Earth = strength, growth, Air = the mind (thoughts flowing through your head) and study. Fire = passion and protection, Water = emotions and healing. Experiment using each of the elements within your candle magick. For example, if you were doing a spell to help with your studying, you could engrave wisps of air into the candle. You could surround your burning candle with something that represents each of the elements, i.e. a stone to represent earth, a feather to represent air, something red or a burning red candle to represent fire and a little bowl of water to the west. Think over what your spell is about and maybe place your candle in the corresponding part of your home (as long as it is safe away from curtains etc.) as appropriate.

Above: each of the elements is assigned to a particular compass direction.

Left: a white candle is used in all candle magick and it represents spirit.

Above: the four elements from left to right; fire (south), earth (north), Air (east) and water (west).

For example, if you are doing a healing spell you may decide to burn your candle in the western part of your home.

I will also be covering other things to take into consideration when performing candle magick so you can combine all of them or simply what you are drawn to – remember, it's your magick and you need to be entirely happy with what you are doing.

A final thought – where would we be without the elements to sustain us? We need the earth to walk upon and feed ourselves, air to breathe, fire from the sun to keep plants growing upon the earth and water for all living things. What other associations can you come up with? To work with the elements is to respect nature, so be of service to our environment and show gratitude for the work they do for us.

Colour affects all of us, in the way we feel or react. Some colours can make us feel energised, other colours help us to relax. Most of us have colours that we like and dislike or colours we are more drawn towards. Businesses involved in selling their goods to the public choose colours that will convey a message about their product to us. Just take a look around you and observe colour. Look at colours used on food packaging – how do the colours they have chosen make you feel about their product? Then imagine the packaging in another colour – would this change the way you feel about that product; would it put you off eating that food? Notice the colours of nature and how they change from season to season. Start to notice what colours other people are wearing – what do you think they say about that person; do you think it reflects the mood they are in?

Colours are so important when performing candle magick. I list their meanings below, for you to take into consideration when choosing a coloured candle for your spell. But, don't feel you HAVE to use the correct coloured candle. For example, if you don't like the colour orange but felt you had to use it for a spell you were doing, whilst you were performing your candle magick you would be putting your dislike of that colour into your magick, and the result may not be as you want!

White candles can be adapted for most spells, so always make sure you have some handy. If you need to do a spell quickly and don't have the colour you need, a white candle will always suffice.

Below: colour affects all of us, in the way we feel or react. Some colours can make us feel energised, other colours help us to relax. Most of us have colours that we like and dislike or colours we are more drawn towards.

WHITE
Purity, truth, cleansing, spirit, peace

BLACK
Banishment, completion, release

GOLD
Autumn, money, attraction, the
sun

SILVER
Overcomes negative energy, the
moon

RED
Summer, energy, activity, passion, sex, life
force, fire, south

ORANGE
Motivation, helps with adapting to different circumstances

PINK
Love, romance, female energies, friendship

YELLOW
Happiness, laughter, concentration, the mind, artistic abilities, air, east

LIGHT GREEN
Spring, fertility, progression, creativity

DARK GREEN
Good luck, strength, growth, good fortune/money, earth, north

LIGHT BLUE
Healing, cooling, calming, vocal expression, water, west

PURPLE/DARK BLUE
Protection, spirituality, psychic abilities, knowledge, water, west

BROWN
Winter, grounding, security, strength, stability, earth

As you can see, different colours, or shades of colours, represent several things. Think of your own interpretations for colours - it's what you feel the colours mean to you when you are doing candle magick that's important.

Try to buy candles that are coloured throughout and not dipped (i.e. white inside).

Also, think about what colour clothes you may want to wear when performing candle magick. You may decide you want to work with your psychic abilities and be protected during your spell so you may choose to wear something purple. Or you may be doing a spell to give you motivation to get some work done, so you could choose to wear yellow. Experiment and have fun!

Left: light green represents creativity among other things and is a good colour for an artistic individual.

Below: yellow is good for a self-employed person as it has many strong qualities which help concentration and the mind,

OILS

Before you even begin to anoint your candle with oil you must ensure the candle is prepared and cleansed of any other influences it may have picked up whilst it was being made or being sold in the shop you bought it from. Please see the section on "Cleansing" for more details.

Oils are used to "anoint" your candle. This prepares both you and the candle for the magick you are going to do. As you rub the oil into the candle, your thoughts must be solely concentrated on the spell itself. Think about the person/people involved, state clearly your intention (remember, with no loopholes!), and clearly state the result you want. Visualise your desired outcome. Play it out as a scene in your head – use your imagination.

Please note that oils must be used carefully. Some essential oils are toxic or can burn the skin if not mixed with a carrier oil or used in the correct quantity. Some oils shouldn't be used if you have certain medical conditions or if you are pregnant, so make sure you follow the instructions provided with the oils you buy.

Firstly, you need to choose an oil that will be appropriate for your spell. You can buy a carrier oil and essences from most chemists, beauty stores or health food shops. Just check to see what they contain – the oil needs to be as pure as possible.

Below: oils are used to "anoint" your candle. This prepares both you and the candle for the magick you are going to do.

I often use good old olive oil as my "carrier oil", which is effective. I then add a few drops of a relevant essence to my olive oil. Here is a list of some of the essences you can add to a carrier oil, along with their meanings:

CHAMOMILE
Health/healing, calming, keeping you balanced and steady

GERANIUM
Harmony, calming and energising, positivity

JASMINE
Sensuality, relaxation, self-confidence, happiness, protection

LEMON
Stimulating, cleansing, removing negative thoughts

ROSE
Love, happiness, contentment

SANDALWOOD
Enhancing meditation and psychic abilities, success

You will find that you can buy oils made from some of the herbs listed elsewhere in this book (see section entitled "Herbs"), therefore follow the same correspondences accordingly. For example, you can rub lavender oil into your candle when you want to do a spell for a friend who has just moved house to bring them blessings in their new home or if you want to help yourself through a stressful situation.

Just add a few drops of the relevant essence to some carrier oil in a small container (please remember to follow the dilution instructions supplied with the essences). If you don't have any of these perfumed oils to hand, don't despair! An anointing oil without scent still works. You could also add some herbs to your base oil (or olive oil) if you wish. Now you are ready to follow the step-by-step guide below to anointing your candle.

Above: good old olive oil is ideal as a "carrier oil"; add a few drops of a relevant essence to it before anointing your candle.

STEP-BY-STEP GUIDE

STEP 1

Place your right hand over the oil container and imagine positive cleansing vibrations flowing out of your hand and into the oil. Imagine that the oil is being washed clean of any negative vibrations and is now completely pure to use in your magick. You can say any words out loud you feel are relevant here.

Once you feel the oil is cleansed, it is time to state its purpose. Once again hold your right hand over the container of oil and say out aloud what qualities the oil needs to impart to your candle. For example, if you were doing a love spell, you may be using rose oil and could say:

May the beauty of the rose attract a suitable love partnership for me, just as the rose attracts the bee.

You need to really concentrate on this for a few minutes until you feel the oil is suitably charged.

STEP 2

Now you are ready to rub the oil into your candle. You need to ensure that before you begin this step your candle has also been cleansed (see page 60), and if you want to engrave any symbols or words into your candle this must be done before the anointing too (see page 34).

Place some oil in your hands (ensure your hands are clean), and rub the oil into the candle starting in the centre and rolling the candle in between your hands to the top near the wick. Then roll the candle from the centre to the bottom of the candle. As you are doing this, you need to be thinking or stating out loud clearly and as simply as possible the details of the spell with your desired outcome (remember leave no room for misinterpretation!).

STEP 3

Once you feel the candle has absorbed your magickal intent (whilst still holding the candle), state out loud:

So mote it be an it harm none.

This simply means that your magick will work if it is meant to be and as long as it harms nobody. (I have written more on this, in the section "What is Magick"?). Place your hands away from and either side of the candle and once again think of your spell and say:

Blessed be.

HERBS

Herbs are very powerful ingredients to use with candle magick. They have been used for centuries in healing and magick. I am listing here some herbs that you should be able to obtain relatively easily, most of which you should find in your kitchen cupboard! You could also grow some of them in pots, window boxes or in your garden. The following herbal associations are for CANDLE MAGICK ONLY and some should not be taken internally without the advice of a qualified herbalist. There are also many books available on herbs and their magickal properties.

Above: herbs are very powerful ingredients to use with candle magick. They have been used for centuries in healing and magick.

ALFALFA
Financial success, creating opportunities

CINNAMON
Good luck, concentration, focus

FRANKINCENSE
Self-confidence, success, cleansing

GINGER
Good health/healing, happiness

LAVENDER
Home blessings, cleansing, calming

LEMON BALM
Love, success, good for studying

MINT
Success, clarity, invigorating

ROSEMARY
Protection, cleansing, remembrance

SAGE
Cleansing, removing negativity

THYME
Love, energising, courage

You could scatter the appropriate herb or herbs of your choice around your candle as it burns.

You could also include the herbs in the anointing oil you rub over the candle.

You could write your desired outcome onto a piece of paper and fold it up after sprinkling the appropriate herb/s into it. Then burn the paper containing the herbs over the flame of the candle. Please ensure if you do this, you are burning the candle in a safe place, away from curtains, tablecloths and other materials.

For instance, burn it in your bath, sink, open fireplace or outside away from dry grass, bushes or plants that may ignite.

It isn't absolutely necessary to perform your magick at a specific time of the day, time of the year or phase of the moon, but it can help. Sometimes you may find it necessary to perform candle magick immediately, without any planning, which is fine. However, sometimes you may want to ensure that everything possible is working with you when you perform candle magick. This section outlines the different periods of time you can use to further empower your magick.

MOON

The moon has four phases - waxing, full, waning, and dark (or new moon). The moon has a feminine energy, whereas the sun is perceived as masculine. I will refer to the moon as "she" as she is associated with many goddess images throughout the world. You will find that some people only recognise three of the moon's phases – waxing, full and waning as they are attributed to the triple goddess and her three phases of maiden, mother and crone. But I believe that we shouldn't forget her when she is resting and waiting for re-birth as this is also a powerful time within her cycle.

A full lunar year has 13 full moons. From full moon to full moon her cycle is approximately 28 days.

The moon affects us immensely. She determines the tides of the sea – oceans and oceans of water. As you will have read earlier in this book, water is linked to our emotions. Therefore the moon can profoundly affect us in this way. Everyone is familiar with the stories of werewolves howling at the full moon! The moon is at full strength at this time, so inevitably she can significantly affect our emotions when she is full. For example, we may have more arguments than usual during a full moon. I believe it has also been noted that more accidents and violent crimes occur at this time, too.

So, what follows are the associations for the four different phases of the moon, so that you can plan your candle magick to work with her powerful energies.

Far left: the moon has a feminine energy, whereas the sun is perceived as masculine.

WAXING

FULL MOON

Far right: when the moon is full she is at her full strength. This is therefore a very powerful time for candle magick relating to fertility.

KEY WORDS: To Fulfil

KEY WORD: Fulfilment

This is when the moon is increasing in strength. She is getting larger and larger. During this waxing phase, she is seen as a maiden, a young girl. Think of what characterises a young girl and you will begin to understand this phase. She has a lot of ambitions to fulfil; she is full of energy, fresh and vibrant; she is growing. Therefore this phase leading up to the full moon is a very auspicious time for doing candle magick to increase something, for growth. You could do a spell to increase someone's health, increase opportunities in your life or increase your will power to get things done! You may decide to do one spell over a period of days during a waxing moon to gradually increase the strength of your spell or bring people together.

The moon is now at her full strength. During this phase she is known as the mother. She is pregnant, full-bellied and strong. She has reached a time of fulfilment and is satisfied with her achievements. She is all woman! This is therefore a very powerful time for candle magick relating to fertility, pregnancy or childbirth. Concentrate on anything that brings fulfilment or abundance. Maybe you have been working hard on a project for some time and you now need to complete it. It is also a good time for focusing on anything to do with creativity.

WANING MOON

KEY WORD: Fulfilled

The moon is diminishing in strength. During this phase she is known as the crone. She is the wise old woman. She knows all, she is fulfilled. This is a good time for candle magick to get rid of anything. You may want to get rid of some old habits or old ways that don't serve you anymore. You could also give healing to someone at this time, to get rid of their disease or illness. It is a good time for cleansing anything and removing negativity.

DARK MOON

KEY WORD: Rest

The moon is now out of sight. She is resting and waiting to be reborn again. This phase can also be known as the new moon, although strictly speaking the new moon is when you see the first, slender glimmer of the waxing moon in the sky. It is at this time she prepares to begin her cycle all over again. This is a fantastic time for doing candle magick to plan for a new beginning. You may want to start a new project, begin a new way of life or make your New Year's resolutions again! This is a good time to think about how you will achieve your goals.

It is a time to rest and recuperate, therefore excellent to focus on bringing about peace. It's also a good time to enhance your psychic abilities, to practise meditation and to search for your soul's desire! If you need to neutralise anything, for example someone may be causing you terrible trouble or they could be dumping their problems on to you, you can make use of this phase.

Below: during a dark moon phase it is a time to rest and recuperate, therefore excellent to focus on bringing about peace.

However, don't worry if you need to do a spell but the moon isn't in the correct phase for the magick you need to perform. Do consider, though, that you can usually fit your magick around her as most situations can be reworded to fit. For example, as explained above, you can do a healing spell during either a waning or waxing moon – waning to rid the person of their illness and waxing to increase their health and strength in order to combat the illness.

As our astrological sign (or sun sign) determines our personality to some degree (i.e. whether you are Leo or Libra), so we also have a moon sign which affects our emotions, our soul and our subconscious. Just as the sun passes into the 12 signs of the zodiac during a year, the moon passes into these same signs on a much more frequent basis. You can buy a moon calendar, which shows what phase the moon is in and which astrological signs she is in day by day for the year.

Above: signs of the zodiac. Just as the sun passes into the 12 signs of the zodiac during a year, the moon passes into these same signs on a much more frequent basis.

DAY OF WEEK	PLANET	TYPE OF SPELL
Monday	Moon	*Psychic abilities, feminine matters, intuition, emotions*
Tuesday	Mars	*Action, sexual matters, courage, war*
Wednesday	Mercury	*Mental abilities, communication, creativity*
Thursday	Jupiter	*Money, success, business/work matters, politics*
Friday	Venus	*Love, fertility, new projects, friendship, beauty*
Saturday	Saturn	*Responsibility, delay, discipline, protection*
Sunday	Sun	*Healing, strength, energy, achievement, ambition*

DAYS OF THE WEEK

Days of the week are linked to the planets. The planets themselves have several areas of influence, which can be researched further. You can therefore plan your candle magick around the days of the week, too. Above is a short list to get you started.

There are many other auspicious times to link your magick to, like planetary hours, the months, the seasons – and also to numerology. Experiment, use your imagination and have fun finding out!

Right: the planet Saturn is linked to Saturday and spells which involve responsibility, discipline and protection.

Gods, goddesses, fairies, nature spirits, unicorns – they all exist! Most religions worship a deity and our history is steeped in them. You may be drawn to Egyptian, Greek or Norse mythologies – there are many more. If you read history or archaeology books within your area of interest, you will find many deities mentioned. It can be fun and very interesting to read about what they stand for, their personalities and who they were, and still are, worshiped by. Find some deities you can relate to. A visit to a museum may hold ancient statues, pieces of jewellery and all sorts of other bits and bobs on which your favourite deities may be depicted. There are many deities, masculine and feminine, for you to get to know. Spend some time with them by meditating on their images. They will come to you in your meditations and give you the opportunity to speak with them. You may at first receive colours, symbols or words – write them all down. These images you are receiving are relevant, so buy yourself a special deity notebook to record your findings in. Over time you will begin to piece together the information you are receiving in your meditations and have your own personal magickal notebook to refer to.

Once you become familiar with the deities, you can dedicate your candle magick to them. For example, if you want to do a love spell, you may wish to dedicate your ritual to the goddess Aphrodite and/or the god Eros. Or for a spell relating to marriage, fertility, childbirth or healing and magick itself, you could call upon the goddess Isis.

Below: most religions worship a deity. You may be drawn to Egyptian, Greek or Norse mythologies, but there are many more to choose from.

Angels are very real and there are many accounts of people seeing them or hearing them speak, especially when people have found themselves in times of danger or have needed guidance or comfort. Once again, you can enjoy finding books, tapes or videos on angels to discover which ones you feel personally in tune with.

So, how about fairies, goblins and unicorns? They exist in a similar way to deities and can be invoked as such. They can usually be called upon to help to protect you during your ritual or to act like messengers and send your magick on its way. You will find, though, that some nature spirits are very mischievous and will lead you a merry dance!

Don't forget fairy tale books, either. You see, the more a fairy story is told the more power is given to it and the more alive they become – a perfect example of what I was saying earlier about the power of the mind. Think of all our imaginations creating these wonderful beings!

I also want to mention animals here, and how they characterise a certain type of behaviour. For example, the wolf is wild, instinctive, powerful, strong and stays as much as possible with its pack. Invoking the wolf would be a good idea for a spell for kinship in your social gatherings, for matters related to your friends or family or for developing your intuition. Take time to consider what different types of animals you are drawn to and what feelings each of them create within you?

Please just remember that these gods, goddesses, angels and nature spirits are very powerful, so treat them with respect and they will be there for you.

Left: fairies, goblins and unicorns exist in a similar way to deities and can be invoked as such.

Far left: angels are very real and there are many accounts of people seeing them or hearing them speak, especially when people have found themselves in times of danger or have needed guidance or comfort.

DECORATING/CARVING YOUR CANDLE

You can also carve your candle before anointing it with oil and burning it. The ritual takes a little bit longer if you include this, but it is fabulous for really enhancing the magickal charge of your candle.

ZODIAC GLYPHS

Aries	♈	Libra	♎
Taurus	♉	Scorpio	♏
Gemini	♊	Sagittarius	♐
Cancer	♋	Capricorn	♑
Leo	♌	Aquarius	♒
Virgo	♍	Pisces	♓

This is where you give free rein to your imagination and carve anything you wish. You can carve words, figures, rune symbols, people's names and star signs, ancient symbols used as talismans and many more. It also makes the magick more personal to you and helps you to really focus on your spell. So, above I have listed a few symbols, above, to get you started.

You can also obtain a photograph of the person you are doing a spell for and cut their body or head out and pin it to the candle. Don't worry – this will not cause harm to the person you are doing the spell for if your intent is good. However, ensure that only the person/people you are working your magick for are cut out – no other people's hands or arms or faces should be seen or you could find the spell doesn't work as you intended! You can place a pin through a certain part of their body to hold the photo to the candle. Choose this position carefully. For example, if a friend of yours has had constant headaches and you are performing a spell to help them get rid of those headaches, you would place the pin through their head, envisaging it releasing the tension there.

Just ensure that when using photos in candle magick you burn your candle in a suitable container as it will burst into flames, so use the smallest photo you have available! Please remember safety at all times.

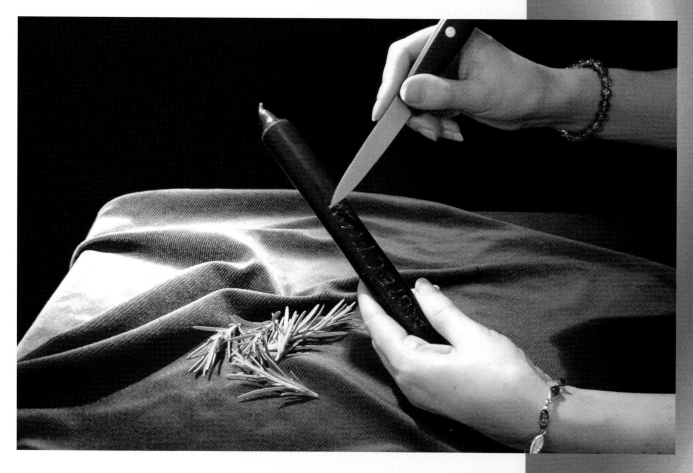

You can also wrap strands of hair around your candle, or add anything else you wish that relates to the spell. You could wrap rose petals around a pink candle for a love spell or draw a mock bank note on a piece of paper and wrap it around the middle of a green candle for a money spell.

Make sure that the implement you are using to carve your candle is safe and isn't likely to cut your finger off! I tend to use a pin. While you are carving your candle you must concentrate on the spell itself, repeating over and over again the details of your spell and your outcome as clearly as you can – the shorter, the better in some cases. You could sing or chant your intent as you are carving – I have included a section on this below. As you carve the candle, your intent flows down your hand, through the knife or implement you are using and deep into the wax.

Above: as you carve the candle, your intent flows down your hand, through the knife or implement you are using and deep into the wax.

CHANTING

As I mentioned in the section on "Decorating/Carving your Candle", reciting your intent by way of chanting or singing can really help. Your imagination feeds on anything like this and therefore raises your inner power, enabling you to keep focused, and you begin to "see" in your mind's eye the manifestation of your desired outcome. All very powerful stuff!

SO WHAT DO YOU CHANT?

Well, you can chant or sing almost anything that helps your magick work. Just keep in mind the spell you are doing throughout.

You can use the words you are using for the spell you are doing. For example you could say:

This spell is for (state person's name) to increase their concentration to achieve all the studying he/she needs in order to pass his/her (state the type of exam) exam.

You repeat this out loud over and over again.

You can repeat the name of a particular deity you are working with.

For example you may be doing a love spell and say

Aphrodite I invite you to be with me and guide me.

You can make up your own poem or words.

This could be something that you say for every spell you do (if appropriate). Just remember to keep focused on the spell in hand! I will share with you one of my little rhymes:

*North, South, East and West,
Help me with the magick,
you know best.
Earth, Air, Fire and Water,
Keep protection at your quarter.*

*May this spell begin to grow,
May the magick begin to flow,
By power of Earth, Moon and Sun.
So mote it be an harm it none.*

Below: you can chant or sing almost anything that helps your magick work. Just keep in mind the spell you are doing throughout.

SO WHEN DO YOU CHANT?

It can be done as you are carving your candle or as your candle burns down. The good thing is that if you need to burn your candle all the way down and you are not going to be near it the whole time (remember the safety tips!), you can chant or sing whilst the candle is out of sight and still provide your spell with continuing power.

SO HOW LONG DO YOU CHANT FOR?

You chant for as long as you like and for as long as it holds your concentration! You will notice that as you chant over and over again your tone will change. Your voice may become louder and louder and you will feel the power rising up within you, getting stronger and stronger. Imagine letting out all of this power from within you and pouring it into the candle. When you feel that your power is at its peak – stop. You don't want to continue chanting past this stage so you become bored or start losing concentration, as this will diminish all of the positive energy you have just created.

Above: as you chant your tone will change and your voice may become louder and louder; you will feel the power rising up within you, getting stronger and stronger. Imagine letting out all of this power from within you and pouring it into the candle.

WHERE DO I BURN MY CANDLE?

You can burn your candle anywhere you feel is appropriate. I find that spells performed outside work extremely well as you are open to the elements that surround you. However, this is not always possible and you need to ensure you will not be disturbed or watched. Candle magick is practically impossible outside anyway, unless you have some glass lamps to burn your candles in so they aren't constantly blown out by the wind! So, to begin with, it would be better to master the art of candle magick indoors!

As mentioned in the section on "Elements", you may wish to burn your candle in a particular compass direction, i.e. the easternmost point of your home or room if the spell has something to do with the element of air and the mind – for example, if you are studying and wish to increase your concentration. If your spell is for money, you could burn your candle in the north.

You may wish to set up your own altar. This is the place where you will cast your spells. It becomes a focal point of your magick and thereby over time becomes a place of power – your personal power. It doesn't have to be constructed upon a large elaborate table. It can be the top of a chest of drawers, a cardboard box, the hearth of a fireplace, a chair or stool – in fact, almost anything will do! Your altar doesn't have to be permanently set up either. However, if you do put it away, make sure you have everything to hand when you need it. You don't want to get into a bad mood trying to find the items for your altar before beginning some magick as you will be creating some inharmonious vibrations – not a good start!

HOW TO CREATE YOUR OWN ALTAR

Firstly decide what you are going to use as your altar. Then find some cloth to cover the surface. You may want to refer to the section on "Colours" and choose a cloth colour according to what magick you will be doing. The cloth on my altar is purple which I chose for added protection and psychic ability. I love this colour and it will not interfere with my magick - whatever spell I may be performing.

Next find items you want to place on your altar to represent the four elements of earth, air, fire and water. – a stone or crystal for earth, a feather or incense for air, a red candle for fire and a little bowl of water (if you can collect water from a natural source, all the better, e.g. rain water or water from a nearby stream). Place the items in their respective positions: earth at the top of your altar for the north; air to your right (the east); fire to the south (the bottom of your altar); and water to your left for the west.

Below: find items you want to place on your altar to represent the four elements of earth, air, fire and water.

Right: you can change your altar with the seasons. Nature will provide you with many wonderful things — a feather, a beautifully coloured leaf, acorns.

Below: you can also represent gods and goddesses with candles: silver for a goddess and gold for a god.

You may also want to include deities on your altar. You could add little statues of gods and goddesses or fairies. Generally speaking, the left side of the altar is for feminine symbols and the right side for masculine symbols.

You can also represent gods and goddesses with candles: silver for a goddess and gold for a god. You could also include pictures of animals, unicorns or seaside or countryside views that you find magickal. Simply place anything on your altar you feel drawn towards. Just be careful not to overload your space so you have no room to perform your spells!

You can change your altar with the seasons. Nature will provide you with many wonderful things – a feather, a beautifully coloured leaf, acorns – just keep your eyes open and they will occur to you. However, do not pick any wild flowers or destroy any form of nature for your altar. You are setting up an altar to work with nature not against it.

You will also need to dedicate some tools for your altar. What will you carve your candles with? What will you light your candles with? (There are differing opinions about whether to light your candle with a lighter or with matches – use whichever you feel drawn towards). What containers will you use for storing or making up your anointing oils and herbs? You don't have to go out and buy these things – you can find them in your kitchen cupboards – but make sure that these items will not be missed! The more natural these items are the better. Maybe you have some wooden bowls or bits of pottery that are suitable. Gather them all together. Make sure they are clean. Place your hands over the items and state in turn what they are to be used for. Imagine power flowing out of your hands into the items as you dedicate them for your magickal work. You will also need to dedicate the item of furniture you will be using for your altar, too. Refer to the section on "Cleansing" for more techniques.

You will also need one white candle to place in the centre of your altar. This represents spirit and is the first candle you light. If you are dedicating your work to a certain deity, light this white candle in their name. Light other candles, including your spell candle, from the flame of this white spirit candle.

Be aware of which direction your altar faces. Refer to the section on "Elements". You may wish to change the direction of your altar according to the spell you are doing. As a general rule if your altar faces north, you work with the power of earth. This is the direction that most altars face, but make up your own mind. My altar faces north, as I usually begin and end my magickal work from the north. I have written more on this in the section entitled "Creating Sacred Space".

Above: you may wish to change the direction of your altar according to the spell you are doing.

YOUR ALTAR IS NOW PREPARED!

It is very important that you are grounded before beginning candle magick. This will prevent strong energies overtaking you and ensures you remain in control at all times. You can tell if you haven't been grounded enough during candle magick, because at the end of your ritual you may feel very light-headed and as if you have your head in the clouds! A good thing to do after performing any candle magick is to eat and drink something. This not only re-grounds you, but you can dedicate your food and drink to any deities you have invoked. It also signifies the end of your ritual and enables you to let go and trust that the spell is now cast and will begin to work its magick. So, here is a step-by-step guide to grounding yourself.

Far left: grounding is very important prior to candle magick and it involves visualisation of the natural world in a very dramatic sense.

Below: when grounding, begin by sitting up straight and comfortably in a chair. Ensure your feet are flat on the ground, your legs and arms uncrossed.

Begin by sitting up straight and comfortably in a chair. Ensure your feet are flat on the ground, your legs and arms uncrossed.

Take a few deep breaths to calm yourself down and begin to relax.

When you feel quiet, still and relaxed, close your eyes.

Now feel your feet flat on the floor. Feel how solid they feel against the floor.

Now visualise roots growing out of your feet and down through the floor/s and into the earth. Don't worry if you can't visualise the roots – just knowing that they are there is good enough.

Imagine your roots growing stronger and thicker. Imagine them growing deeper and deeper into the ground.

Imagine your roots spreading out deep within the earth. You begin to feel securely rooted to the spot!

Now see if you pick up any sensations from the earth. Is the earth warm or cold? Dry or moist? Can you smell the earth? Really imagine what it feels like to be a tree rooted to the spot. The earth is your stability and security; it cares for you; it nourishes you.

Far left: imagine what it feels like to be a tree rooted to the spot. The earth is your stability and security; it cares for you; it nourishes you.

Left: take long, slow deep breaths and, as you do so, imagine drawing up all that wonderful earth energy through your roots and into your body.

Now you are ready to breathe up the earth into your body. Take long, slow deep breaths and, as you do so, imagine drawing up all that wonderful earth energy through your roots and into your body. Imagine the earth energy flowing up your legs, torso, hands and arms, up your neck and to the top of your head.

Release your breath, imagining sparkling white light flowing down through the top of your head all the way back down through every part of your body and down through your roots and back into the earth.

Repeat this three times.

Now take a few seconds, even minutes if you wish, to regulate your breathing until you feel entirely relaxed and still.

Reaffirm to yourself that you are securely grounded – you are feeding on the earth's nourishment and you are feeling secure, relaxed, calm and steady.

Now you are ready to open your eyes and begin your magickal work! You would normally follow this by creating your sacred space, so that's what I shall talk about next.

CREATING SACRED SPACE

To ensure you are working in harmony with the elements, with no negative or disruptive vibrations affecting your magick, you need to create sacred space. Some would argue that it isn't absolutely necessary to create sacred space, but I always do. I have also found that, so far, I have never been disturbed once my sacred space has been created. So I personally feel you need to create sacred space every time you cast a spell. In the end it is entirely your decision as to whether it feels right for you or not — trust your intuition.

Right: creating sacred space is about inviting the elemental guardians to watch over your magickal work.

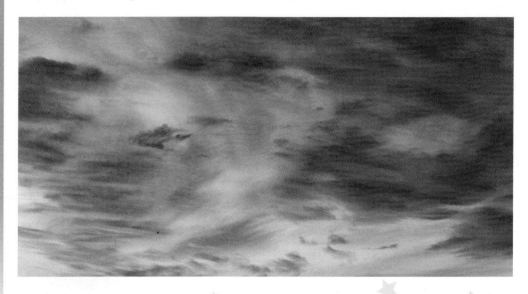

Creating sacred space is about inviting the elemental guardians to watch over your magickal work, to keep you safe and protected and to create a "clean" environment (i.e. the banishment of negative energies). After your magickal work is complete you also "banish" or disperse the sacred space by thanking the elements for their guidance and protection and saying goodbye. There are several ways of creating sacred space. Firstly I will describe here a generally accepted version, but I use a different method, which I will share with you later. Over time you will find out other ways — just go with what feels right for you.

There will be occasions when you will need to perform candle magick quickly, without any planning, and so one way is to simply say a rhyme out loud calling on the elements. Other times you may want to put an entire evening aside to perform your candle magick and indulge yourself with a more formal or lengthy method. I use both methods accordingly.

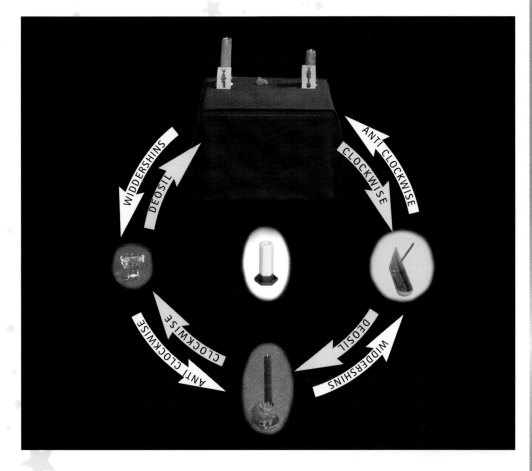

The direction you take to walk or dance around your sacred space is important. Clockwise, otherwise known as deosil, increases the power and energy – it creates. Anti-clockwise, otherwise known as widdershins, releases the power and energy – it banishes.

To begin with you will need items to represent each of the elements – for example, a stone, crystal or bowl of salt for the north/earth; some incense or a feather for the east/air; a red candle or a symbol of the sun for the south/fire; a small bowl of water or a sea shell for the west/water. You don't have to stick to these suggestions. If you find something else you would like to use instead that represents these elements – great!

You will also need to know where north, south, east and west are in relation to where you will be performing your candle magick. If you are not absolutely sure of these directions – use a compass!

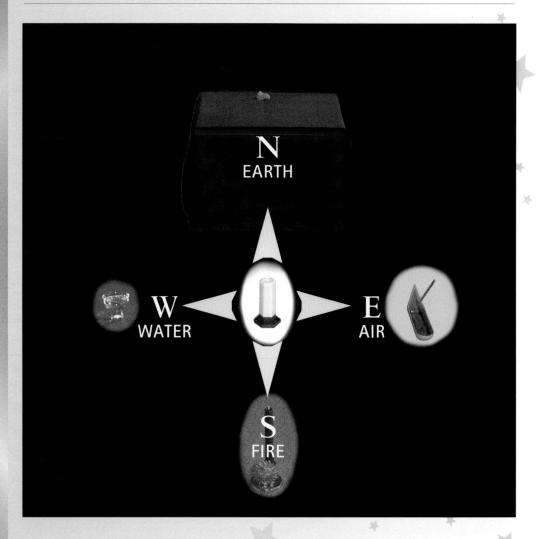

Right: place your elemental items in their respective places in a circle around you. Make the circle large enough for you to stand in the middle, so that you have enough room to perform your candle magick.

You will also need a white candle. This candle represents spirit.

If you are using an altar, place this at the northernmost edge of the circle where your item representing the element of earth will be.

Place your elemental items in their respective places in a circle around you. Make the circle large enough for you to stand in the middle, so that you have enough room to perform your candle magick. Also ensure you can move around the outside of the circle, too, and that you are not hemmed in by any other pieces of furniture.

Make sure the items you have chosen for your elements, your white candle and any other tools you will be using are cleansed (see page 60). Place the white candle in the centre of the circle and stand behind it, Do not light it at this point.

Ground yourself (see page 43).

Begin by lighting the white candle in the centre of your circle. Fully focus your mind on the work you are about to do.

Now walk to the east and face outwards (with your back to the candle in the centre of your circle) and walk around clockwise, pointing your index finger (of the hand you write with) around the edge of the circle. Imagine pure white light streaming out of your finger and creating a sphere of protection all around you.

Walk around the circle visualising this three times, ending in the east. Take a moment or two to visualise as much as you can so that you are comfortably encased within your sphere of white light. It acts as a protection all around you, above and below you.

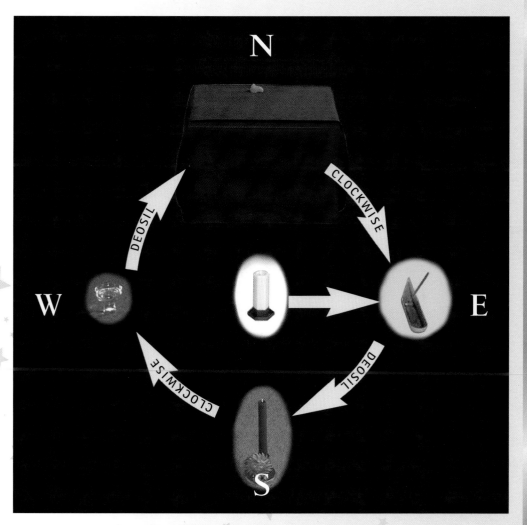

Above: the white candle, which is placed in the centre of your sacred space represents spirit.

Left: walk to the east face outwards and walk around clockwise, pointing your index finger (of the hand you write with) around the edge of the circle.

Below: if you are using incense, you will need to light this from the spirit candle in the centre of your circle.

Pick up your incense, feather or other item you are using to represent air. If you are using incense, you will need to light this from the spirit candle in the centre of your circle. Walk clockwise around the circle, returning to the east and saying:

Guardian spirits of the east, spirits of air, I ask that you be here to witness my rites and protect my circle. Hail and welcome.

Replace your item that represents air on the ground to the east.

Repeat in the same way turning next to the west and saying:

Guardian spirits of the west, spirits of water, I ask that you be here to witness my rites and protect my circle. Hail and welcome.

Then walk clockwise to the south. If you are using a red candle to represent fire, light it from the spirit candle in the centre of your circle. As before, walk clockwise around the circle, ending back in the south saying:

Guardian spirits of the south, spirits of fire, I ask that you be here to witness my rites and protect my circle. Hail and welcome.

Right: if you are using a red candle to represent fire, light it from the spirit candle in the centre of your circle.

You then end with the north in exactly the same way as before, saying:

Guardian spirits of the north, spirits of earth, I ask that you be here to witness my rites and protect my circle. Hail and welcome.

If you are using salt for the north and water for the west, you can sprinkle these around your circle as you say the above words. Then simply return to the east to complete the circle (you do not need to say anything more to the east).

Now you are ready to invoke the god or goddess and any other deity you wish. Focus your attention upon the white candle in the centre of your circle. Say:

I call upon the goddess. I call upon the god. I invite you both to be present here now to witness, bless and guide me throughout my magickal work. Hail and welcome.

You may decide to call upon a particular aspect of the god and goddess here, related to the spell you will be performing. For example, in a love spell you may call upon the goddess Aphrodite and the god Eros. In this case, state their names as appropriate:

I call upon the goddess Aphrodite. I call upon the god Eros....

Below: in a love spell you may call upon the goddess Aphrodite and the god Eros.

Below left: when you are ready to invoke the god or goddess and any other deity you wish. Focus your attention upon the white candle in the centre of your circle.

If you want to invoke the guardianship and guidance of any animals, fairies, angels or whatever else to join you, do so now in your own words. Ensure that the words you use and your intentions towards them are respectful. Imagination is the key here – visualise and sense their presence around you. Make sure, however, that whichever aspect of the god or goddess or whichever animal, fairy or angel you invite, they are harmonious to the spell you will be doing, or you could be in for a surprise – and not always a good one!

Right: if you want to invoke the guardianship and guidance of any animals, fairies, angels, or whatever else to join you, imagination is the key here – visualise and sense their presence around you.

Spend a few moments standing before your spirit candle, feeling the presence of the deities you have invoked.

Now you are ready to perform your candle magick.

If you need to leave your sacred space at any time, cut an imaginary door in the side of your protective sphere of light. Make sure that you re-seal it behind you. Do the same when re-entering the space.

After you have performed your candle magick, you will need to "banish" or clear your sacred space. I don't really like the word banish as it implies you have no regard or respect for the power of the elements or deities you have invoked, which is why I tend to use other words like "clear". This is an opportunity to thank the elements and say goodbye with love and respect. You simply do this the same way you created your sacred space, but you extinguish any burning elements, i.e. incense or your red candle. Here's how it's done:

Stand at the east and hold the object that represents this quarter. Say:

Guardian spirits of the east, spirits of air, thank you for your presence, guidance and protection. Hail and farewell.

If you are using incense, extinguish it now.

Then move to the south (remembering to extinguish your candle if you are using one) and repeat as before, continuing to the west and the north. Move to the east to complete the circle.

Below: after you have performed your candle magick, you will need to clear your sacred space which involves extinguishing the burning elements in your sacred space.

Now it is time to say goodbye and thank you to the god and goddess and any other deities you have been working with. Walk to your spirit candle in the centre of your circle. Take a few moments to think about how the spirits have helped you during your magickal work. Then extinguish the spirit candle, saying:

God and goddess, thank you for your presence here. Thank you for your guidance and protection. Hail and farewell.

Remember to use their names if you have invoked a particular aspect of them. Follow this by saying the same to any other animals or deities you have invoked.

Right: to say goodbye and thank you to the god and goddess and any other deities you have been working with. Walk to your spirit candle in the centre of your circle. Take a few moments to think about how the spirits have helped you during your magickal work. Then extinguish the spirit candle.

Your sacred space is now cleared.

As I mentioned at the beginning of this section, there are many other ways of creating sacred space. I said I would share with you the way I prefer so that you can see the difference between the two.

I use all the items as mentioned before, but also include a silver candle for a goddess and a gold candle for a god.

I place my altar at the north.

I do everything the same from the beginning as mentioned above, up to and including lighting the white spirit candle, but this is placed in the centre of my altar.

I begin creating my sacred space from the north, not the east as in the example above.

The rest of the process is the same as I walk around to each element in a clockwise direction, but here are a few different words you could use for each of the quarters:

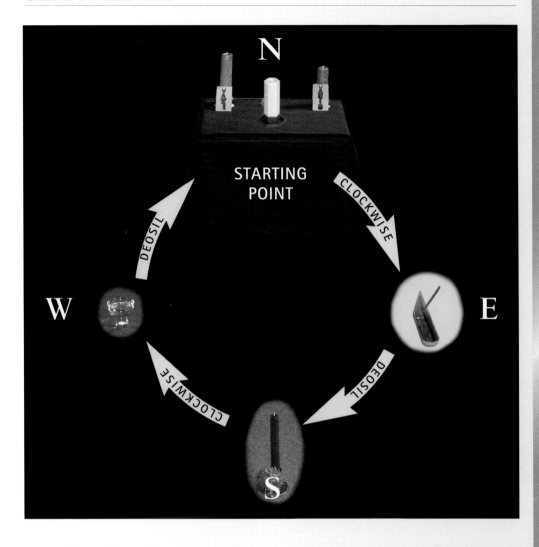

Left: a spirit candle placed in the centre of an alter at the north of the circle. In this arrangement North becomes an alternative starting point to creating your sacred space.

Guardian spirits of the north, spirits of earth, I invite you to be present here now to guide me and protect me during my magickal work. May you provide me with your strength and stability. May you create dense thorny bushes that will prevent negative energies from drawing near and may the gentle beauty of your nature bring forward positive energies. Guardian spirits of the north, hail and welcome.

Guardian spirits of the east, spirits of air, I invite you to be present here now to guide me and protect me during my magickal work. May you provide me with clarity of mind. May your strong winds prevent negative energies from drawing near and may your gentle loving breeze bring forward positive energies. Guardian spirits of the east, hail and welcome.

Far right: a sacred space set up on an alter — an alternative if there is no room to make a full size circle.

Guardian spirits of the south, spirits of fire, I invite you to be present here now to guide me and protect me during my magickal work. May you provide me with your strength and true passion bringing precise action to my work. May your raging fires prevent negative energies from drawing near and your loving warmth bring forward positive energies. Guardian spirits of the south, hail and welcome.

Guardian spirits of the west, spirits of water, I invite you to be present here now to guide me and protect me during my magickal work. May you provide me with harmonious emotions and flowing love. May your powerful waves prevent negative energies from drawing near and your calming gentle waters bring forward positive energies. Guardian spirits of the west, hail and welcome.

Don't feel that you need to keep strictly to the set words — make up your own expressions, as long as you keep in tune with the elements. Ask for guidance and protection and say "hail and welcome".

After calling in the west I move to the north to complete the circle. This brings me to my altar and I stand before it. The silver candle is at the top of the altar on the left and the gold candle at the same level to the right.

I now call in the god and goddess separately. I light the silver candle when calling in the goddess and the gold candle when calling in the god. My words change all the time as I invoke different aspects of the god and goddess as appropriate to the magick I am performing. So use your imagination, know what "person-alities" the god and goddess aspects carry and don't be afraid to ask for their guidance accordingly. But you can simply use the words:

I call upon the goddess. I invite you here to be present now to witness, bless and guide me throughout my magickal work. Hail and welcome.

You can create your sacred space to suit your surroundings. If you do not have the room to create a large circle in which you can walk around, create your sacred space on a table top or as part of the altar.

Above: use pictures of the deities or gods that you are calling on, Alternatively use something you have found which represents them.

Light the silver candle from the white spirit candle as you say:

Hail and welcome.

Use the same words for the god and light the gold candle in the same way as the silver.

If I am calling in any other deities or animals, I may have a picture of them on my altar or something I have found that represents them. You could also use a candle. For example, if you wanted to ask for the strength of the lion you could use a red candle for fire as this represents the element under which the star sign Leo falls.

I clear my sacred space in a different way, too. I begin at the west and work anti-clockwise to the north. I feel I achieve some form of balance doing it this way. Firstly I am moving both clockwise and anti-clockwise, and secondly I am calling in the elements forwards and backwards in the same order:

North, East, South, West

and clear in the reverse order:

West, South, East, North.

I use similar words to the first example for saying thank you and goodbye.

I then say goodbye to the god and goddess and any other deities in the same way as mentioned before.

So what are my reasons for beginning and ending at the north/earth I hear you ask? The north is the direction of the earth's powerful energy life force

– the life force that gives us the body to walk upon this earth. I worship mind, body and spirit, but feel that my body is a very important tool in performing this ritual. I therefore incorporate dance and various other physical techniques appropriate to the work in hand.

I do work with the spirit during the ritual (inviting the god and goddess and other spiritual beings) and with the mind (through visualisation and focus upon the work being performed). But sometimes I feel that we can forget how important our bodies are in expressing spirituality. There will be those of you who disagree with this, which is fine. We are all individuals – bless the god and goddess for that!

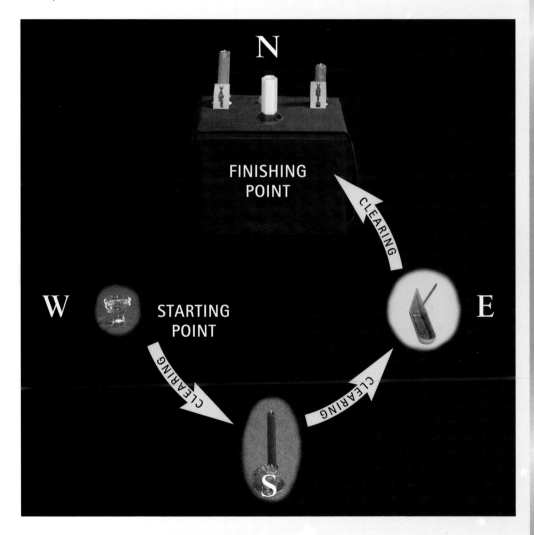

Left: when clearing a sacred space, which has the alter at the north with the white spirit candle in the centre of it, move in an anti-clockwise direction starting at the west and finishing at the alter in the north.

CLEANSING

You need to ensure that any items you will be using whilst performing candle magick are cleansed of any unwanted negative energies. This will obviously prevent these energies having a detrimental impact upon your magick. Once cleansed, your items will be "virgin" for you to work with as intended. I will describe here two ways of cleansing your items. You will come across other ways, too. Once you become used to cleansing your tools, you will find your own preferred method. Just ensure that any candle you use for magick is a new one each time. Never use the same candle for two or more different spells.

Once again your visualisation and imagination are important here. So enjoy and go with the flow!

Firstly you need to ensure that the item is physically clean by removing any dust or dirt.

Before you begin your cleansing ritual, ensure you are grounded (see page 43).

Hold the item you wish to be cleansed in both of your hands. Close your eyes and concentrate on the item for a few minutes and see if you can begin to feel its vibration. Don't worry if you can't – it will come to you in time. With your eyes still closed and keeping this image firmly in your mind, ask that the god and goddess come forth to cleanse this object (you may ask in your mind or out loud).

Below: any items you will be using whilst performing candle magick need to be cleansed to prevent any negative energies they have picked up from interfering with your candle magick.

Left: hold the item you wish to be cleansed in both of your hands. Imagine silver and gold light streaming from between the palms of your hands into the object. Imagine these colours swirling around inside the object and radiating outwards until the whole object is encased in gold and silver light.

Imagine silver and gold light streaming from between the palms of your hands into the object. Imagine these colours swirling around inside the object and radiating outwards until the whole object is encased in gold and silver light. Imagine these colours banishing all negativity and absorbing it to be transformed into positivity. Keep going with this visualisation until you feel the whole object is cleansed and now vibrating with positive energy. Once you feel this is complete (and be patient it may take a few minutes!), imagine pure white light streaming from between your palms and into the object. When you are ready, open your eyes.

Your item is now cleansed and ready to use.

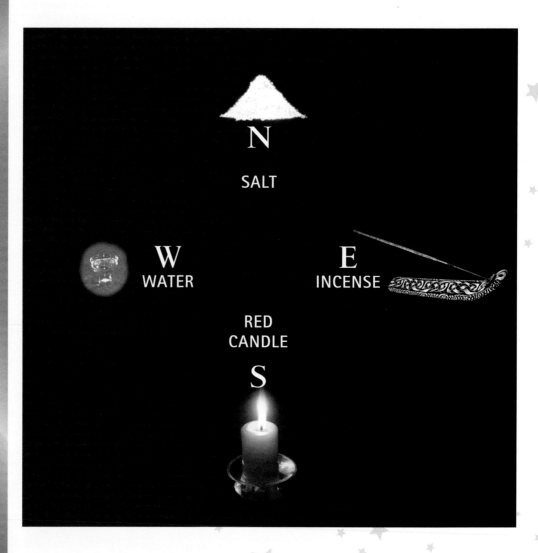

The other method of cleansing your tools is by passing them through each of the elements. In order to do this you must firstly create sacred space using salt for the north, incense for the east, a red candle for the south and a bowl of water (preferably from a natural source) for the west. In the directions below, I have combined a cleansing and charging ritual. Charging your tools is like charging up a battery, empowering your tools to begin their appropriate work.

Hold the object in between your hands and feel its vibration (as above).

Next go to the west to sprinkle and rub your object with water, saying three times:

I wash clean this tool with water (sprinkle with water). May any energies be banished from this tool that do not work in harmony with my magick (sprinkle with water). I charge thee in the name of the god and goddess (sprinkle with water).

Then turn to the south and pass your tool through the flame of the red candle three times, saying:

I burn away to cleanse this tool with fire (pass through the flame). May any energies be banished from this tool that do not work in harmony with my magick (pass through flame). I charge thee in the name of the god and goddess (pass through the flame).

Then turn to the east and pass your tool through the smoke of the incense three times, saying:

I blow away to cleanse this tool with air (pass through the incense smoke). May any energies be banished from this tool that do not work in harmony with my magick (pass through the incense smoke). I charge thee in the name of the god and goddess (pass through the incense smoke).

Finally turn to the north and rub your tool with salt three times, saying:

I cleanse this tool with earth (rub with salt). May any energies be banished from this tool that do not work in harmony with my magick (rub with salt). I charge thee in the name of the god and goddess (rub with salt).

There is nothing wrong with performing both of these cleansing rituals – in fact it will enhance them if you do.

Below: pass your tool through the flame of the red candle in the south, three times, as part of the cleansing process.

I have put together some candle magick spells to get you started. So set aside some time when you will not be interrupted and enjoy creating your own magick! I would recommend that you read through the spell first before performing it, so that your attention will not drift and your spell will flow much more naturally.

Don't worry if you do not have any of the "optional extras" mentioned in the spells. They really are optional extras and the spell won't need them to succeed.

Before you begin each spell you will need to make certain preparations as follows:

Firstly gather together everything you will need on your altar or within easy reach of where you will be performing your candle magick. Make sure that all these items are cleansed (see page 60). If you keep your representations for the elements together somewhere safe and only use them for this purpose, you will normally only need to cleanse these once. Place your representations of the elements in a circle around you in their appropriate places: salt (earth) at the north, incense (air) at the east, red candle (fire) at the south and water at the west.

Far left: if you keep your representations for the elements together somewhere safe and only use them for this purpose, you will normally only need to cleanse these once.

Below: unless stated otherwise, the spell candle must be left to burn down completely, extinguishing itself naturally. So ensure your candle is left in a safe place. Never leave it unattended as it could fall over and set fire to something. It is also a good idea to choose a spell candle which is not too large – which could take days to burn down completely!

You will be performing your candle magick inside this circle, so ensure you have enough room and that everything you need is within the circle. If you are using an altar, place this at the northernmost edge of your circle where you place the salt. Your white spirit candle is in the centre of your circle (or centre of your altar), and if you are using the gold and silver candles for the god and goddess place these either side of your spirit candle – silver to the left and gold to the right.

Unless stated otherwise, the spell candle must be left to burn down completely, extinguishing itself naturally. So ensure your candle is left in a safe place. Never leave it unattended as it could fall over and set fire to something. If you do need to leave it alone, for example overnight, I recommend leaving it to burn down in a sink, in a fireplace with the fireguard in front of it, or in the bath. Even better, place it near a smoke alarm! Make sure the candle holder is not made of glass or anything that is likely to catch fire or melt. You can occasionally return to watch your candle burning down and repeat any rhymes or chants you said in your ritual, or simply visualise your desired outcome again. But once the candle has burnt itself out, it's time to forget the spell.

Left: it is a good idea to buy a notebook specifically to write your spells in and for your comments on how the spell worked.

It's a good idea to buy a notebook specifically to write your spells in and for your comments on how the spell worked – take note of any unexpected results and learn from them! Be absolutely positive in your mind that your spell will succeed. If you forget it, the spell can be left alone to work its magick!

Make sure that if you use herbs in your anointing oil that there are not large pieces which could ignite. Crush them as much as you can.

I think that's all the preparation and warnings out of the way – so, let's get on with it!

A SPELL TO BRING LOVE TO YOU OR SOMEONE ELSE

YOU WILL NEED

Pink candle
White candle
Anointing oil
Pin or something to carve your candle with
Matches/lighter
Representation for the north
Representation for the east
Representation for the south
Representation for the west
A strand of your hair, or the person's hair you are doing the spell for

OPTIONAL EXTRAS

Gold and silver candle for the god and goddess
Rose oil
An appropriate herb, i.e. thyme, lovage, lemon balm

TIMING

Waxing moon
Friday

Make your preparations as described below.

Ground yourself (see page 43).

Create your sacred space up to the point where you call in the god and goddess as you will be doing this slightly differently (see page 46).

When you call in the god and goddess for this spell, you will be calling upon their aspects that represent love. I have chosen the Greek goddess Aphrodite and the Greek god Eros. So, as you focus your attention upon the spirit candle (or as you light the silver and gold candles), say:

I call upon the goddess Aphrodite. I invite you to be present here now to witness, bless and guide me throughout my magickal work. I honour your beauty. Come enjoy your involvement in this spell of love. Hail and welcome.

I call upon the god Eros. I invite you to be present here now to witness, bless and guide me throughout my magickal work. Fly to me on your golden wings and shoot your magickal arrow into the heart of this spell of love. Hail and welcome.

FRIDAY

Far left: a love spell set up in a sacred space on an alter. Using a pink rose and petals as an extra touch as well as the god Eros and goddess Venus.

Spend a few moments thinking of the god and goddess.

Now you need your pink candle. Hold it, close your eyes and feel its vibration. Concentrate on the reason for your love spell and the outcome you desire.

Now it's time to begin carving your candle. Carve a love heart at the top of the candle. Then carve your name (or the name of the person who has requested you to do this spell for them) and date of birth, next to the heart running lengthways towards the bottom of the candle. Place another love heart at the end of the candle, so you have love hearts either side of your name. As you do this, visualise yourself (or the person you are doing the spell for) surrounded in a pink light.

Right: carve a love heart at the top of the candle. Then carve your name (or the name of the person who has requested you to do this spell for them) and date of birth, next to the heart running lengthways towards the bottom of the candle.

You now need to focus solely and intently upon the desired outcome of this spell. On the opposite side of the candle to where you have written the name and date of birth, you need to carve a few symbols that relate to the outcome. Keep focused on this throughout by chanting or singing one of the following (or you could make up your own rhyme):

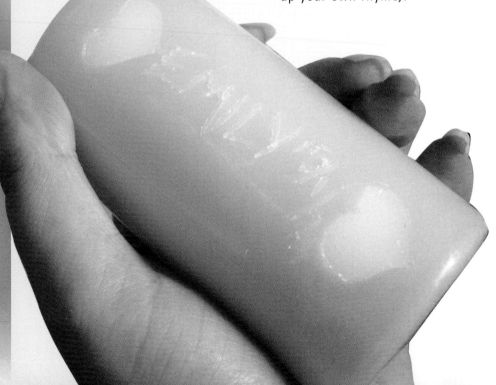

IF YOU ARE PERFORMING THE SPELL FOR SOMEONE ELSE

Bring two together.
Both desire true love.
Both desire each other.

IF YOU ARE PERFORMING THE SPELL FOR YOURSELF

Just as the rose attracts the honey bee,
Bring my one true love to me.

Carve two hearts entwined at the top of the candle.

Carve an "X", a runic symbol for partnership, at the bottom of the candle.

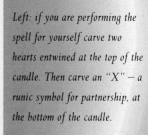

Left: if you are performing the spell for yourself carve two hearts entwined at the top of the candle. Then carve an "X" – a runic symbol for partnership, at the bottom of the candle.

Now it's time to anoint your candle. Follow the directions on page 20 It is at this point that, if you have it, you can add a few drops of rose oil or herbs to your anointing oil (olive oil will be fine). Whilst anointing your candle you still need to be focused on your desired outcome, so chant the little rhyme I mentioned earlier in this book:

North, South, East and West,
Help me with the magick, you know best.
Earth, Air, Fire and Water,
Keep protection at your quarter.

May this spell begin to grow,
May the magick begin to flow,
By power of Earth, Moon and Sun.
So mote it be and it harm none.

Visualise as much as you can that you (or the person you are doing the spell for) are receiving a loving relationship. Now I should mention at this point that it would not be right to state anyone else's name here as regards getting two specific people you know together. That would be altering one or both of their minds to do something they do not wish to do. In the long term this would not lead to a happy relationship. Also, do not say anything to the effect that the two specified people are together forever – you may regret it at a later date and be stuck with them forever as you asked! Leave room for free will.

Once you have anointed your candle, take a strand of hair and wrap it around the middle of the candle. Now place it in a stable candle holder either in the middle of your altar or the middle of your sacred space (next to your spirit candle). You could now sprinkle some more love herbs if you have them around the base of your candle. Sprinkle them in a clockwise direction starting at either the east or the north as you wish.

Say out loud:

I cast this spell to bring true love for me (or state person's name) as soon as is right to be so. Aphrodite and Eros help me towards this aim. So mote it be an it harm none.

Then light your candle from the white spirit candle. You could also, even though they are alight, touch the wick to the god and goddess candle flames. Sit and concentrate on your spell once more. You may like to dance clockwise around your circle of sacred space envisaging power entering your burning candle. Be with your candle, concentrating on your desire for as long as you wish.

When you are ready, clear your sacred space (see page 53).

Leave your candle to burn out by itself. Follow the safety guidelines.

May cupid shoot his golden arrow to the target of your desire!

Above: Cupid; a very useful god to call on during a love spell.

A SPELL FOR MONEY

Be aware that this spell could simply bring you opportunities for earning money. Be careful how you phrase things, too – if you simply ask for money, you may receive it through an unlucky circumstance. For example, you may receive a disastrous haircut and the hairdressers will pay you compensation, or you may be burgled and receive insurance money, or worse still you may receive an inheritance as a result of someone's death. On a lighter note, you could use this spell to bring luck to your lottery ticket or if you are entering any other competition to win money!

Above: be aware that this spell could simply bring you opportunities for earning money.

THURSDAY

YOU WILL NEED

Green candle
White candle
Anointing oil
Pin or something to carve your candle with
Matches/lighter
Representation for the north
Representation for the east
Representation for the south
Representation for the west

OPTIONAL EXTRAS

Gold and silver candle for the god and goddess
Sandalwood oil
Mint (either oil or the plant itself)
An appropriate herb, i.e. alfalfa, cinnamon
Lottery ticket or competition details/entry form

TIMING

Waxing moon
Full moon
Thursday

Make your preparations as described above.

Ground yourself (see page 43).

Create your sacred space and call in the god and goddess and any other animals or deities you wish. If you want to call in the god and goddess separately, do so by lighting the silver candle for the goddess and the gold candle for the god (see page 56).

Hold your green candle, feel its vibration and say three times:

Green candle of prosperity,
more money for me there soon will be,
not through ill or misfortune.
Bring me the money soon, soon, soon.

You now need to carve the three following words and symbols into the green candle. Say the above rhyme once for each symbol or phrase you carve:

£... the amount of money you require (enough for your needs – don't be greedy, your spell may not manifest!)

Money to me.

The runic symbol for Fehu (for possessions).

Far left: a spell for money using cinnamon, mint to help with the success of the spell.

Below: the runic symbol for Fehu (for possessions).

Below: carve the three following words and symbols into the green candle. £... the amount of money you require (enough for your needs — don't be greedy, money to me and the runic symbol for Fehu.

Carve over the top of them twice more. Repeat the above rhyme each time you carve over a symbol. So at the end of the carving you will have said the rhyme a total of nine times.

After carving your symbols, hold the candle and close your eyes. Visualise yourself receiving the money you have asked for and thank the god and goddess.

Now anoint your candle (see page 20). If you choose to, you could add sandalwood oil, mint, alfalfa or cinnamon to your anointing oil.

Place your anointed candle in a stable candle holder either in the middle of your altar or the middle of your sacred space next to your spirit candle.

If you have a lottery ticket or completed competition entry form or details, place this under your candle holder now.

If you wish, you could now sprinkle some more herbs, if you have them, around the base of your candle. Sprinkle them in a clockwise direction starting at either the east or the north as you desire.

If you have a lottery ticket or completed competition entry form or details, place this under your candle holder now.

If you wish, you could now sprinkle some more herbs, if you have them, around the base of your candle. Sprinkle them in a clockwise direction starting at either the east or the north as you desire.

Next place your hands either side of the candle and say out loud:

I cast this spell to bring good fortune my way (state the amount of money you require) as is right to be, through no misfortune or loss to me or anyone else. May only good come of this spell for all involved. So mote it be an it harm none.

Really think about these words and what they mean. Then light your candle from the white spirit candle. You could also, even though they are alight, touch the wick to the god and goddess candle flames. Sit and concentrate on your spell once more. You may like to dance clockwise around your circle of sacred space envisaging power entering your burning candle. Be with your candle, concentrating on your spell for as long as you wish.

When you are ready, clear your sacred space (see page 53).

Leave your candle to burn down by itself. Follow the safety guidelines.

May prosperity be yours!

Below: if you have a lottery ticket or completed competition entry form or details, place this under your candle holder.

FRIDAY

Below: during the peace spell call in the help of a white dove. visualise it flying in a light blue sky; let your imagination take over and let the dove show you what peace is.

A SPELL FOR PEACE

You can use this spell as you see fit. You may want to do your bit to help bring peace to a place of unrest somewhere in the world, bring peace to your home if everyone seems to be arguing or bring peace to a friend in distress.

YOU WILL NEED

Two white candles (and candle holders)
Anointing oil
Pin or something to carve your candle with
Matches/lighter
Small pot of salt for the north
Incense for the east
Red candle (and holder) for the south
Small pot of water for the west

OPTIONAL EXTRAS

Gold and silver candle for the god and goddess
Chamomile, geranium, jasmine, lavender or rose oil
An appropriate herb, i.e. sage, ginger, lavender
Picture of a white dove

TIMING

Waxing, waning or dark moon
Friday

As in previous rituals, fully prepare everything for your spell by placing your elements around you and setting up your altar or space in the centre of your circle.

Place the candle holder for your spell candle only, at the eastern quarter, next to your incense.

Ground yourself (see page 43).

Create your sacred space and call in the god and goddess.

This time you will call in the help of a white dove. Stand in the centre of your circle holding your white spell candle and close your eyes. Visualise a beautiful white dove flying in a light blue sky. Imagine it's a warm and peaceful day. Look around you – you are in beautiful countryside; there are

flowers everywhere. Let your imagination take over and let the dove show you what peace is. You may feel the need to dance or move your body as you connect to this beautiful bird. Spend as long as you like with the dove, but make sure that when you open your eyes you feel peaceful and happy.

Once you have opened your eyes, sit down in the centre of your circle and carve whatever words or symbols you feel drawn towards that relate to your spell. Here are some suggestions: peace, harmony, calm, ending of war in (state name of place), serenity.

Left: carve into your white candle whatever words or symbols you feel drawn towards that relate to your spell.

As you do this you need to state the intention of your spell appropriate to the phase of the moon you are in. Here are some examples:

WAXING MOON

State that this spell will bring peace to the situation. The desire for peace will increase and take hold.

WANING MOON

State that this spell will rid the situation of anger, violence, war etc. and thereby bring peace.

DARK MOON

State that this spell will help people to realise that the unrest is no longer achieving anything, that it is a time to rest, and that justice will bring a peaceful way of life.

After carving your symbols, hold the candle and close your eyes. Visualise the peaceful situation relating to your spell. Imagine those people you are doing the spell for receiving love and peace. Act out a scene in your head. When you are ready, thank the god and goddess and the dove of peace. Open your eyes.

Now anoint your candle (see page 20). If you choose to, you could include some of the oils and herbs listed in the "optional extras" list above.

Holding your anointed candle, face east and sit or stand by your incense. Pass the candle through the smoke of the incense three times whilst saying:

Air flow, air blow
peaceful winds of change.

Then turn to face south and pass the candle through the flame of your red candle three times whilst saying:

Fire calm, fire's warmth
Be still and gently rest.

Next turn to the west and sprinkle the candle with droplets of water three times whilst saying:

Cool waters, healing waters
soothe troubled emotions.

Lastly, turn to the north and sprinkle the candle with salt three times whilst saying:

Mother nature, the magick of nature
bring peace on earth.

Now return to the east and place your candle in its holder (which you have placed in this quarter).

Far left: after carving your symbols, hold the candle and close your eyes. Visualise the peaceful situation relating to your spell.

Right: you could sprinkle some more herbs, if you have them, around the base of your candle. Sprinkle them in a clockwise direction starting at either the east or the north as you wish.

Then return your spell candle to the middle of your altar or the middle of your sacred space next to your spirit candle.

You could now sprinkle some more herbs, if you have them, around the base of your candle. Sprinkle them in a clockwise direction starting at either the east or the north as you wish.

Say out loud:

I cast this spell to bring peace and love as is right to be, to (state here the reason for your spell). May only good come of this spell for all involved. So mote it be an it harm none.

Really think about these words and what they mean. Then light your candle from the white spirit candle. Imagine as you do so the white wings of the dove flapping and sending out your spell to the universe. As before, if you wish, you can touch the lighted wick of your spell candle to the lighted candles of the god and goddess. Sit and concentrate on your spell once more. You may like to dance gracefully, clockwise around your circle of sacred space, imagining you are the dove of peace. But keep the peaceful nature of your spell in your dance. Otherwise, you could sit and close your eyes and go through the visualisation you did at the beginning, walking in the countryside and watching the dove. Be with your candle, concentrating on your desire for as long as you wish.

When you are ready, clear your sacred space (see page 53).

Leave your candle to burn down by itself. Follow the safety guidelines.

Peace be upon you!

Well, I hope that you have now got the general idea of how to perform candle magick. I am now going to suggest a few more ideas for spells. You are armed with all the knowledge you need in this book, so enjoy making up your own rituals. Remember, they can be as simple or as complicated as you like!

HEALTH SPELL

TIMING

Waxing moon (to increase strength)
Waning moon (to get rid of illness or disease)
Sunday

COLOUR

Light blue
Red

NEVER use the colour green for a healing spell involving cancer as this colour represents growth.

If someone is going to be ill over a period of days, you could burn a candle for them as each day passes. Place a photograph of them under the candle of when they were happy and healthy.

If someone is ill but needs to continue working for a while, burn a red candle along with a blue candle. You may be able to find a candle which has both of these colours in it. The red candle signifies the physical strength and energy they need to keep going, whilst the blue candle will hopefully prevent them from getting any worse.

Engrave the person's name on the side of the candle along with words like "health and vitality" and "healing".

For the waxing moon, write their name and date of birth on a piece of light blue paper, along with appropriate words for their healing, and burn it in the candle flame.

For the waning moon, write their name and date of birth on a piece of white paper, signifying cleansing, and burn it in the candle flame.

SUNDAY

Far left: if someone is ill but needs to continue working for a while, burn a red candle along with a blue candle.

Below: for the waxing moon, write their name and date of birth on a piece of light blue paper, along with appropriate words for their healing, and burn it in the candle flame.

Right: use incense for this spell as it represents air and the mind, preferably frankincense as this relates to self-confidence and success.

Below: find a photograph of yourselves when you were happy and good friends. an wrap it around the candle, securing it with a pin ad yellow or pink cotton.

To Heal a Broken Friendship

Timing

Dark moon
Wednesday (to bring communication if you haven't been speaking)
Friday

Colours

Pink (friendship)
Yellow (communication)

Find a photograph of yourselves when you were happy and good friends. This photograph preferably needs to be when you were standing side by side, linking arms or generally close to one another. If you don't have a photo of this, you can cut out different photos of each other and stick them together with a pin, which will attach the photo to the candle. Write any words, symbols or your desired outcome of this spell on the back of the photo with either a yellow or pink pen. Attach your photo securely to the candle with a pin and wrap some pink and/or yellow cotton around it. Ask that past differences be dissolved.

CREATIVITY

TimING

*Full moon
Wednesday*

Colours

Yellow

Use incense for this spell as it represents air and the mind, preferably frankincense as this relates to self-confidence and success. But maybe you need help with expressing yourself with more clarity, or bringing more energy to your creativity, in which case include mint in your candle magick.

Write down the help you need on a piece of yellow paper, and fold into it some pieces of mint. Burn this piece of paper in the candle flame.

Or simply keep the piece of paper and mint under your candle until it burns all the way down and then go outside and bury it in the ground.

You could also place the piece of paper under your pillow at night and ask that you receive guidance in your dreams.

WEDNESDAY

Below: write down the help you need on a piece of yellow paper, and fold into it some pieces of mint. Burn this piece of paper in the candle flame.

SATURDAY

PSYCHIC PROTECTION

TIMING

Waxing moon
Dark moon

COLOURS

Purple
Dark blue

If you feel under psychic attack or someone is directing negative energy your way, any spell that strengthens your psychic self defence will help to keep harm at bay.

The most effective way of dealing with psychic protection would be to cleanse yourself BEFORE working on psychic protection. Burn a sage stick around you or hold some sage in your left hand, imagining it is cleansing you. Take a salt bath. Burn a white candle for your cleansing.

For this spell you will need to burn a purple or dark blue candle. If you wish , carve words and symbols into the candle whilst chanting; repeating a few words over and over again.

*Protection above, below
and around me.*

You can then do the following.

Use jasmine or rosemary as part of your anointing oil or sprinkle jasmine flowers or sprigs of rosemary around your candle in a clockwise direction.

Use some lemon if you need to help yourself to think more positively.

Here is a visualisation technique you can follow which builds up a self-defence barrier around you. Do this whilst burning your dark blue or purple candle within sacred space.

Sit quietly and ground yourself.

Close your eyes and take three deep breaths.

Imagine something growing up from under your feet, encircling you (clockwise) and over the top of your head. This could be a brick wall, a glowing purple or dark blue light which forms a bubble around you, a thorny hedge or anything else you are drawn towards. Paint a sign on the front of your brick wall, for instance, stating:

NEGATIVE ENERGIES NOT PERMITTED.

or visualise the purple or dark blue light glowing outwards from your bubble and pushing away anything negative. In the case of the thorny hedge or anything else you are visualising, you need to ensure that negative energies are kept away and only positive energies are allowed in. Use your imagination and visualise placing symbols, colours or personal items within your boundaries.

The only thing you must ensure is that this protection goes under your feet, over your head and around your body so it completely surrounds you. This will now go with you wherever you are. Take a few minutes each day to sit quietly and reaffirm your protection.

A reminder: if you send out negative energies or perform magick that goes against anybody's will, you will be leaving yourself open to comeback – no matter how much protection you give yourself. What goes around comes around!

I hope you have enjoyed reading this book and it has helped you to understand candle magick a little better. Carry on experimenting with different herbs, oils and various other techniques. You will soon be a master at the art. I wish you success!

Blessed be!

Far left: the most effective way of dealing with psychic protection would be to cleanse yourself BEFORE working on psychic protection; take a salt bath. Burn a white candle for your cleansing.

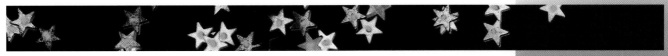

SAFETY PAGE

Try at all times to be with your candle as it burns down. Never leave it unattended.

If you HAVE to leave your candle unattended, please ensure your safety by placing it somewhere it can burn safely.

Ensure that, if the candle falls over, it will not set light to anything else in the vicinity.

Leave it to burn down in a shower cubicle, the bath or a sink with some water in the bottom of it. Alternatively, leave it in your fireplace with the fireguard safely in position.

INDEX